AF375274

HARMONY'S PATH

Harmony's Path

POEMS OF LOVE, NATURE, AND SERENITY

Angela Hart Aldridge

AHARTBOOKS

Harmony's Path: Poems of Love, Nature, and Serenity

LOVE AND ROMANCE

Eternal Flame

In the heart's quiet chamber, a spark ignites,
A flame that dances with the rhythm of two souls' delights.
Through whispered promises and tender caresses,
Love blossoms, eternal, defying earthly stresses.

In the twilight's embrace, our spirits entwine,
A symphony of passion, a melody divine.
With every heartbeat, our love takes flight,
A beacon in the darkness, a guiding light so bright.

In the garden of love, we plant seeds of hope,
Nurtured by laughter, in life's vast scope.
Through the seasons' traverse, our bond grows strong,
A mosaic of memories, where we both belong.

With each sunrise, a new chapter unfolds,
A canvas of dreams painted in striking bold hues.
In the tapestry of time, our love we'll proclaim,
Forever burning bright, our eternal flame.

IN YOUR EYES

In the depths of your gaze, I find my repose,
A sanctuary where our love freely flows.
In the language of your eyes, tales unfold,
Love's silent symphony, a story untold.

In the mirror of your soul, reflections sway,
A kaleidoscope of emotions at play.
Through life's endless stream, our hearts align,
In your eyes, I find solace, a love divine.

In twilight's embrace, our spirits take flight,
A journey of two souls, bathed in starlight.
With each beat of our hearts, a tale untold,
In your gaze, forever, our love shall hold.

In night's silence, our love speaks its truth clear,
In whispers of love, void of doubt or fear.
For in your eyes, my true self I see,
Bound by love's embrace, forever free.

So let the world fade, in time's fading light,
In your gaze, our love shines ever bright.
For within your eyes, I find my youth,
In our love's infinity, eternal truth.

Sunrise Serenade

In the soft embrace of dawn's first light,
We stand together, hearts taking flight.
Beneath the canvas of the waking sky,
Your hand in mine, our spirits high.

As the sun paints hues of gold and pink,
We share a moment, no words to think.
In the quiet stillness of this morn,
Our love renewed, forever born.

As the world awakens to the morning's kiss,
We savor the sweetness of love's gentle bliss.
With each breath of air, a promise untold,
In the sunrise serenade, our hearts enfold.

In the soft whispers of the morning breeze,
We find solace in nature's harmonies.
With each beat of our hearts, a symphony,
In the sunrise serenade, our souls set free.

As the day unfolds its vibrant hues,
We cherish the moments, fleeting but true.
With each passing second, our love grows,
In the sunrise serenade, where passion flows.

In the dance of light upon the land,
We find ourselves, hand in hand.
With each step we take, the world transforms,
In the sunrise serenade, where love reforms.

So let us linger in this moment divine,
As the sun ascends, our souls align.
In the soft embrace of dawn's first light,
In the sunrise serenade, our love takes flight

Everyday Bliss

In the simple moments, life unfolds,
As we navigate its twists and holds.
With you by my side, each day's a treasure,
Finding joy in life's simple pleasures.

From morning coffee to shared laughter,
Every moment with you, ever after.
In the rhythm of our daily dance,
Our love finds its sweet romance.

In the simple moments, life unfolds,
As we navigate its twists and holds.
With you by my side, each day's a treasure,
Finding joy in life's simple pleasures.

From morning coffee to shared laughter,
Every moment with you, ever after.
In the rhythm of our daily dance,
Our love finds its sweet romance.

In the warmth of your smile, my heart finds rest,
Every touch, every glance, by love we're blessed.
In the quiet moments, just us two,
Everyday bliss, in all that we do.

With each sunrise, a promise renewed,
In the bond of our love, forever pursued.
Through the highs and lows, together we stand,
Everyday bliss, hand in hand.

First Date Frenzy

Nerves flutter, anticipation high,
As we prepare for our first try.
In the mirror, we check our attire,
Heart racing with the flames of desire.

From the moment our eyes first meet,
Every word and smile feels sweet.
In this moment, time stands still,
As we embark on this thrilling thrill.

Nerves flutter, anticipation high,
As we prepare for our first try.
In the mirror, we check our attire,
Heart racing with the flames of desire.

From the moment our eyes first meet,
Every word and smile feels sweet.
In this moment, time stands still,
As we embark on this thrilling thrill.

Conversation flows, like a gentle breeze,
As we navigate this first date with ease.
Laughter fills the air, hearts beating fast,
Moments like these, destined to last.

With each shared glance, a connection grows,
In the warmth of the night, love surely shows.
As we bid farewell, under the moonlit sky,
Our first date frenzy, a memory to defy.

Love's Enduring Glow

Through the sands of time, our love does flow,
Ever steady, a constant glow.
In the face of trials, we stand strong,
For our love, an eternal song.

Though years may pass and seasons change,
Our bond remains, steadfast and unchanged.
In the depths of our hearts, it will always stay,
Love's enduring flame, come what may.

Though years may pass and seasons change,
Our bond remains, steadfast and unchanged.
In the depths of our hearts, it will always stay,
Love's enduring flame, come what may.

In moments of joy and times of sorrow,
Our love shines bright, today and tomorrow.
Through every storm, we'll weather the blow,
For in each other's arms, love's enduring glow.

With every sunrise and each sunset's hue,
Our love deepens, ever true.
In the tapestry of life, our story we'll sew,
With threads of devotion, love's enduring glow.

Destined Souls

In the fabric of fate, our threads entwine,
Destined to meet in space and time.
From the moment our souls first touched,
We knew our love was always much.

Through the trials and triumphs we've faced,
Our connection never once displaced.
For in each other's arms, we find our home,
Destined to roam, together we'll roam.

With every step, our journey unfolds,
In the story of us, our love beholds.
Through every twist and turn, our hearts align,
Destined souls, forever entwined.

Hand in hand, we traverse life's winding road,
Together we'll weather every heavy load.
Through stormy seas and skies of blue,
Our love guides us, pure and true.

In the echoes of laughter and tears we've shed,
In every word whispered, and every vow said,
Our souls resonate with a love profound,
In the silence of hearts, our connection is found.

With each passing day, our bond grows strong,
In the melody of love's eternal song.
For in the tapestry of our intertwined fate,
Our love shines bright, never to abate.

So let us cherish every moment we share,
In the embrace of love, beyond compare.
For in this dance of destiny, our souls unite,
Destined to love, in eternal light.

Lost in Your Embrace

In the warmth of your arms, I find my peace,
As the world around us seems to cease.
Lost in the depths of your loving gaze,
In your embrace, I'm lost in a haze.

Every touch, every whispered word,
Echoes the love that's felt and heard.
In this moment, nothing else matters,
Lost in your embrace, my heart forever flatters.

With every heartbeat, a symphony plays,
In the rhythm of love, our souls ablaze.
Wrapped in the cocoon of your tender care,
Lost in your embrace, beyond compare.

In the silence of night, our spirits entwine,
In the sanctuary of love, yours and mine.
Lost in the eternity of this tender space,
In your embrace, I find my grace.

So let the world spin on, in its endless race,
For in your arms, I've found my place.
Lost in your embrace, forever I'll dwell,
In the haven of love, where all is well.

Unconditional

In the garden of our love, flowers bloom,
Each petal a testament to love's sweet perfume.
For in your eyes, I find my reflection,
In your love, there's no exception.

Through the highs and lows, thick and thin,
Our love remains, a constant win.
In your arms, I find my sanctuary,
For your love, unconditional, is my reality.

With each passing day, our bond grows strong,
In the melody of love, we belong.
Through stormy weather and sunny skies,
Your love, unwavering, never dies.

In the garden of our hearts, seeds of trust,
Blossom into a love, pure and just.
For in your embrace, I find my home,
In your love, unconditional, I'll roam.

So let the world spin on, in its endless chase,
For in your love, I find my grace.
In the garden of our love, forever I'll stay,
With you by my side, come what may.

Gratitude's Song

For every smile, for every tear,
For every moment we hold dear.
I thank you, my love, for all you do,
For being my rock, for seeing me through.

In your support, I find my strength,
In your encouragement, I find my length.
For every dream you help me chase,
In your love, I find my grace.

With each sunrise, with each sunset's glow,
In your love, gratitude I show.
For the laughter shared, for the tears we've shed,
In your embrace, my heart finds stead.

For the light you bring into my life,
For being there through joy and strife.
In your presence, my heart sings along,
For you, my dear, this gratitude's song.

Love's Tapestry

Every love story, unique and true,
A masterpiece painted, just for two.
In the tapestry of life, our threads entwine,
Creating a love story, yours and mine.

Through twists and turns, ups and downs,
Our story unfolds, with every sound.
For in the beauty of our shared lore,
Our love finds its forevermore.

In every color, in every hue,
Our love's palette, ever anew.
With each stitch, with every line,
Our love's tapestry, one of a kind.

Through stormy weather and skies so clear,
Our love's fabric, unwavering, sincere.
For in the pattern of our embrace,
Our love weaves a tale of grace.

So let us cherish each woven strand,
In our love's tapestry, hand in hand.
For in the threads of our hearts' design,
Our love's masterpiece, eternally shines.

Obstacles Overcome

In the face of challenges, we stand tall,
Together, we conquer, we never fall.
For in the power of our love's embrace,
Obstacles crumble, leaving only grace.

Through storms and tempests, we prevail,
With love as our compass, we set sail.
For in the journey of love's grand scope,
Obstacles dissolve, leaving only hope.

With every trial, we grow stronger,
In the depths of love, we linger longer.
For in the bond that binds our souls tight,
Obstacles fade, in love's radiant light.

In the echo of triumph, our hearts sing,
With every obstacle, a new beginning.
For in the dance of life, we find our way,
Obstacles overcome, in love's sweet sway.

MARRIAGE AND COMMITMENT

MARRIAGE AND COMMITMENT

Everlasting Vows

Beneath the arch of skies, we pledge our hearts,
Bound by love's covenant, unbreakable and true.
Through valleys low and mountains high, hand in hand,
Together we journey, forever me and you.

In the whispers of the wind, our promises soar,
A melody of devotion, forevermore.
With every step, our love strengthens its hold,
In the tapestry of eternity, our story's told.

Through the trials of time, our bond remains,
An unyielding fortress against life's pains.
For in each other's arms, we find our home,
In the sacred vows we made, we'll never roam.

The Dance of Years

In the tapestry of time, our story unfolds,
Each thread woven with laughter, tears, and gold.
Through seasons of joy and storms that test our might,
We dance through life's rhythm, side by side, day and night.

In the ballroom of life, we twirl and we sway,
Each step a testament to love's endless play.
With every heartbeat, the music grows strong,
In the dance of years, our love's lifelong song.

Through moments of triumph and trials we face,
We embrace the dance with elegance and grace.
For in the steps we take, we find our delight,
In the timeless waltz of love, forever in flight.

Forever Mine

In the dance of love, we found our way,
Two souls entwined, come what may.
With every step, our bond grew strong,
In the melody of love's sweet song.

Through laughter and tears, we've grown old,
In the warmth of love, our hearts enfold.
For in the promise of forevermore,
We find peace, our souls to adore.

In the journey of marriage's embrace,
We find joy, in every trace.
For in the depths of love's sweet wine,
I am yours, forever mine.

Hand in hand, through life's parade,
In love's sanctuary, our hearts are laid.
For in the promise of eternity's shine,
I am yours, and you are mine.

Unity's Song

In the symphony of marriage, our hearts unite,
Two souls entwined, in love's pure light.
With every promise spoken, our bond does grow,
In the dance of forever, our love shall show.

Through the trials we face, hand in hand we stand,
In the strength of our union, we understand.
For in the sanctuary of marriage's embrace,
We find solace, in love's endless grace.

In the echoes of vows, our spirits soar,
In the harmony of love, forevermore.
For in the melody of unity's song,
We find belonging, where we belong.

Together Forever

In the garden of marriage, our love does bloom,
With every season, our hearts find room.
Through the laughter and tears, we endure,
In the promise of forevermore, we're sure.

Hand in hand, through life's winding trail,
In the echoes of love, we'll never fail.
For in the tapestry of marriage's embrace,
We find strength, in love's endless grace.

In the canvas of life, our story unfolds,
In the warmth of love, our hearts behold.
For in the journey of together forever,
We find joy, our souls to sever.

Bound in Love

Bound in love's embrace, our hearts are tied,
In the covenant of marriage, side by side.
With every promise, our love does grow,
In the journey of forever, we'll go.

Through the storms we weather, our love prevails,
In the shelter of marriage's endless trails.
For in the depth of love's sweet surrender,
We find peace, in love's tender.

In the symphony of marriage's song,
Two hearts beat as one, lifelong.
For in the rhythm of love's sweet rhyme,
We find solace, in love's prime.

Forevermore

In the tapestry of marriage, our story we weave,
With every moment shared, our love does cleave.
Through the highs and lows, we stand as one,
In the promise of forever, our journey begun.

Hand in hand, through life's journey we stride,
In the warmth of love, our hearts confide.
For in the sanctuary of marriage's vow,
We find strength, in love's sacred now.

In the melody of forevermores' song,
Our hearts entwined, lifelong.
For in the promise of eternity's shine,
We find solace, in love's divine.

NATURE WITH LOVE

Summit Serenade

Atop the world, where mountains kiss the sky,
We stand as one, beneath the heavens high.
With every step, our love climbs ever higher,
A journey of two souls, ignited by desire.

In the whispers of the wind, our dreams take flight,
As we scale the peaks, bathed in golden light.
With each summit conquered, our spirits soar,
In the summit serenade, forevermore.

Through valleys deep and canyons wide,
We journey together, side by side.
With every obstacle, our love's strength unfurled,
Guided by passion, in a boundless world.

On the summit's crest, where the air is clear,
We share whispered vows, without a fear.
In the vast expanse, our love takes flight,
In the echo of our laughter, in the morning light.

Trail of Love

Hand in hand, we tread the winding trail,
Through valleys lush and peaks that pierce the veil.
Amidst nature's grandeur, our love finds its stride,
Boundless and free, like the mountain's endless tide.

In the rustle of leaves, our laughter sings,
As we traverse the path, on adventurous wings.
With every step, our love's journey unfolds,
In the trail of love, where our destiny molds.

Through forests dense and meadows fair,
We wander together, without a care.
In the embrace of nature, our love blooms bright,
Guided by stars, in the gentle night.

Beside cascading waterfalls and tranquil streams,
We share whispered secrets, as if in dreams.
In the embrace of solitude, our hearts entwine,
Forever connected, in nature's design.

Ocean's Embrace

In the embrace of the ocean's azure hue,
We lose ourselves in moments pure and true.
Amidst the whispers of waves and the sun's gentle caress,
Our love blooms anew, in the sand's soft embrace.

In the dance of the tide, our hearts entwine,
As we stroll hand in hand, in rhythm divine.
With every wave that kisses the shore,
Our love deepens more and more.

Beneath the canopy of the endless sky,
We share secrets and dreams, you and I.
In the symphony of nature, our souls align,
Entwined forever, in love's sacred shrine.

With the salty breeze caressing our skin,
We find solace in the moment, within.
In the vastness of the ocean, our love sails,
With each wave's embrace, our bond never fails.

Footprints in the Sand

Along the shore, where white sands meet the sea,
Our footprints merge in perfect harmony.
In the ebb and flow of tide, our love remains,
Etched forever in the sands of time's endless plains.

In the grains of sand, our memories reside,
As we walk together, with love as our guide.
With each footprint left behind in the sand,
Our love's story echoes, forever grand.

In the whispers of the breeze and the ocean's call,
We find solace together, standing tall.
In the silence of the beach, our love whispers sweet,
Forever entwined, in each other's heartbeat.

As the waves wash away our prints with the tide,
Our love remains steadfast, side by side.
In the dance of the ocean and the sun's warm glow,
Our love's eternal footprint, forever it will show.

Tranquil Forest

In the heart of the forest, silence reigns,
A sanctuary where the soul reclaims.
Amongst the towering trees, serenity found,
In nature's embrace, where peace is bound.

Beneath the canopy, whispers are heard,
A gentle rustle, like a soothing word.
In the dance of light, through leaves it plays,
In the tranquil forest, where spirits raise.

The breeze carries tales of ancient lore,
Whispered secrets from those who came before.
In the rustle of leaves, stories untold,
In the heart of the forest, where mysteries unfold.

Birdsong breaks the silence, a symphony pure,
Each note a melody, rich and sure.
In harmony with nature, their songs unite,
In the tranquil forest, where dreams take flight.

Creatures of the wild find solace here,
In the sanctuary of the forest, free from fear.
Their footprints weave a story on the forest floor,
In the tranquil forest, where all can explore.

Spring's Symphony

In the garden of spring, colors bloom,
As fragrant blossoms chase away the gloom.
With every petal, a melody sung,
In nature's chorus, where hearts are strung.

The air is alive with the buzz of bees,
As they dance from flower to flower with ease.
Their hum a harmony in the symphony of spring,
In the garden of life, where hopes take wing.

The gentle patter of raindrops on leaves,
A rhythm that nature joyfully perceives.
In the rejuvenation of earth, life's pulse beats strong,
In the garden of spring, where new beginnings belong.

The sun's warm embrace brings life anew,
As it bathes the world in a golden hue.
Its rays a conductor, guiding nature's show,
In the garden of spring, where wonders grow.

Starry Night Sonata

Beneath the cloak of the night's dark veil,
Starry constellations tell their tale.
In the endless stretch of the cosmic domain
We find solace in its mystery.,

The Milky Way stretches across the sky,
A river of stars that catches the eye.
Its beauty transcends time and space,
In the starry night sonata, we find our place.

The moon, a silent guardian in the night,
Casts its glow with a soft, silver light.
Its phases a reminder of life's ebb and flow,
In the starry night sonata, where dreams aglow.

Shooting stars streak across the sky,
A fleeting glimpse as they pass by.
Their beauty a reminder of life's fleeting grace,
In the starry night sonata, where time and space embrace.

Autumn's Waltz

In the dance of autumn, leaves take flight,
A kaleidoscope of color, burning bright.
With every gust of wind, a gentle sway,
In nature's waltz, we find our way.

The crunch of leaves beneath our feet,
A rhythm that nature's dance repeats.
In the symphony of rustling leaves,
In autumn's waltz, our heart believes.

The scent of cinnamon and spice,
A fragrance that lingers, oh so nice.
In the crispness of the air, a refreshing chill,
In autumn's waltz, we feel a thrill.

The harvest moon rises in the sky,
Casting its glow with a gentle sigh.
In its light, we find a sense of peace,
In autumn's waltz, where troubles cease.

Blossoming Growth

In the heart of a flower, secrets hide,
As petals unfurl, revealing life's tide.
With every bloom, a story unfolds,
In nature's garden, where dreams take hold.

The gentle unfurling of a rose,
A beauty that nature freely bestows.
In its petals, the promise of a new day,
In the heart of a flower, where dreams find a way.

The vibrant colors of a field in bloom,
A tapestry of life, dispelling gloom.
In the midst of chaos, beauty is found,
In nature's garden, where love is profound.

The buzz of bees, the flutter of wings,
A symphony of life that nature brings.
In the heart of a flower, life's melody,
In blossoming growth, where hearts are free.

Thunderous Reverie

In the roar of thunder, nature's voice,
A symphony of power, with no choice.
With every bolt of lightning, a flash of light,
In nature's fury, where day turns to night.

Dark clouds gather, in a dramatic display,
The sky alive, in its own wild way.
In the thunderous reverie, nature's might shown,
In awe we stand, in its presence alone.

The rumble of thunder, a deep bass note,
Echoing across the sky, nature's anecdote.
In its wake, the scent of rain on dry earth,
In the thunderous reverie, where life finds rebirth.

The crack of lightning, a brilliant flash,
A moment frozen in time, in its bash.
In the symphony of storms, nature's grand design,
In the thunderous reverie, where power aligns.

Resilient Beauty

In the face of adversity, nature thrives,
With strength and grace, it truly survives.
Through trials and tribulations, it stands tall,
In nature's resilience, we find our call.

The sturdy oak withstands the strongest gale,
Its roots deep in the earth, it will not fail.
In its branches, the story of resilience,
In nature's beauty, where strength is immense.

The delicate flower, fragile and fair.

HEARTBREAK AND LOSS

Fragments

Fragments of memories, shards of our past,
Scattered like leaves in the tempest's fierce blast.
Amidst the ruins of what once was so dear,
I gather the pieces, each one a silent tear.

In the quiet of night, your absence echoes loud,
A haunting melody that pierces through the shroud.
Yet in the depths of darkness, a flicker of light,
The promise of dawn after the longest night.

In the labyrinth of sorrow, I search for a sign,
A glimpse of solace, a reason to shine.
Though the road is long and the journey steep,
I'll gather the fragments, no matter how deep.

For in the mosaic of pain, there's beauty to find,
A kaleidoscope of memories, intertwined.
Though broken, I'll rise, stronger than before,
For love's true essence, forevermore.

Echoes of Departure

In the quiet of night, your absence echoes loud,
A haunting melody that pierces through the shroud.
Yet in the depths of darkness, a flicker of light,
The promise of dawn after the longest night.

In the silence of solitude, memories replay,
Echoes of departure, in the stillness they sway.
A symphony of longing, in the heart's lonely beat,
In the absence of presence, your absence, complete.

But in the hush of dawn, hope begins to rise,
A whisper of tomorrow, painting the skies.
For in the quiet of night, though you may depart,
Your essence lingers on, forever in my heart.

Through the mist of morning, I find my way,
In the echoes of departure, I learn to stay.
For though you may leave, your love remains,
In the echoes of departure, forever it reigns.

Cherished Memories

In the corridors of my mind, you reside,
A beacon of light, in memory's tide.
With every thought, a cherished embrace,
In the echo of your laughter, I find solace.

Memories dance like fireflies in the night,
Each one a treasure, a guiding light.
In the silent whispers of moments past,
Your presence lingers, forever to last.

Though you've left this world, you're never far,
In the memories we hold, like a guiding star.
For every laugh shared and tear shed,
In cherished memories, you'll always tread.

Farewell, Beloved Companion

With tearful eyes and heavy heart,
I bid farewell, we must part.
Your paw prints forever etched in my soul,
As I relinquish your earthly role.

In the quiet corners of my heart, you'll stay,
A faithful companion, along life's way.
Though your presence may no longer roam,
Your love endures, guiding me home.

With each step I take, I'll carry you near,
In the memories we shared, forever dear.
Though your absence leaves a void so deep,
In my heart's embrace, your love I'll keep.

Bittersweet Farewell

In the bittersweet embrace of goodbye,
I release you, my heart's heavy sigh.
For in letting go, we find our peace,
As memories linger, never to cease.

Your presence, a melody that stills the night,
A symphony of love, pure and bright.
Though our time together now must end,
In the heart's embrace, you'll forever mend.

Through tears of sorrow, love's light shines through,
In the bittersweet farewell, I find you.
For though you've left this earthly plane,
In love's eternal dance, we remain.

Lessons in Loss

In the depths of sorrow, wisdom blooms,
As grief's tendrils weave through life's rooms.
With every tear shed, a lesson learned,
In loss's embrace, our souls yearn.

Through pain and anguish, we find our strength,
In loss's wake, we journey the length.
For in the darkness, light still shines,
Guiding us through the hardest times.

In the tapestry of life, loss finds its place,
A thread woven with love, and grace.
For though we grieve, we also grow,
In the lessons of loss, our hearts aglow.

Echoes of Longing

In the silence of night, I call your name,
Hoping to hear your voice, just the same.
But the echo of emptiness fills the air,
As I long for the touch of your care.

In the quiet moments, memories flood,
A river of longing, a tide of blood.
For though you're gone, you're never far,
In the echoes of longing, where you are.

With each passing day, the ache remains,
A testament to love, bound by chains.
Yet in the stillness of the night's embrace,
I find solace in your lingering grace.

Legacy of Love

In the legacy you left behind,
A tapestry of love, endlessly kind.
With every life touched, your impact shown,
In the hearts you've touched, forever known.

Your presence lingers in the lives you've touched,
A legacy of love, that's never brushed.
For though you're gone, your spirit remains,
In the hearts of those, who still proclaim.

Through acts of kindness and words of grace,
You left a mark, that time can't erase.
For in the legacy of love you've sown,
Your spirit lives on, forever known.

Mother's Embrace

In the silence of night, I feel your gentle touch,
A whisper of love from the heavens above.
Though you've parted from this world, your spirit soars,
In every song of birds and the wind's soft roars.

In the depths of my soul, your love resides,
A guiding light in life's tumultuous rides.
With each passing day, your memory stays,
In the mother's embrace, that never strays.

In the memories we cherish, and the lessons we've learned,
Your love remains steadfast, forever returned.
In the beauty of nature and the songs of the dove,
We find solace and peace, in your eternal love.

In the garden of memories, we walk hand in hand,
As your spirit surrounds us, like grains of sand.
In the embrace of love, we find our way,
Forever guided by your light, come what may.

Healing Journey

Through the labyrinth of grief, we tread,
With each step forward, our hearts led.
In the healing embrace of time's gentle hand,
We find peace in the journey's land.

Though the road is long and the path is steep,
In healing's embrace, we find release.
For with each sunrise and each setting sun,
We find solace in what's done is done.

In the journey of healing, scars may remain,
A testament to the strength we've gained.
But with each step forward, we find our way,
In the healing journey, day by day.

Loss's Natural Course

In the cycle of life, loss finds its place,
A natural rhythm, we must embrace.
With every goodbye, a hello anew,
In loss's ebb and flow, love's residue.

Though we may stumble and we may fall,
In loss's embrace, we stand tall.
For with every ending, a beginning starts,
In the cycle of life, where love imparts.

Through loss and grief, we find our way,
In the natural course, day by day.
For though we mourn what's gone before,
In loss's cycle, love endures.

Love's Eternal Embrace

In the shadow of death, love's light shines bright,
A beacon of hope in the darkest night.
For though you're gone, your love remains,
In the heart's eternal flame, it sustains.

Through the passage of time, your love endures,
In the heart's embrace, forever pure.
For though you've left this earthly plane,
In love's eternal embrace, you remain.

Though we may part, in body and in form,
In love's eternal embrace, we're reborn.
For though you're gone, you're never far,
In love's eternal embrace, where you are.

Life's Eternal Dance

In the tapestry of life, we play our part,
Each step a testament to love's enduring art.
Though shadows may fall and tears may flow,
We carry on, for love's light will always glow.

In the dance of life, we find our way,
Through the darkest nights and the brightest day.
With each twirl and sway, we embrace the unknown,
In life's eternal dance, love's legacy is shown.

In the laughter of children and the touch of a friend,
In the memories we cherish, until the very end.
In the beauty of sunrise and the calm of the night,
We find strength and courage, in love's guiding light.

In the tapestry of time, our love is weaved,
In every moment cherished, every dream achieved.
In the embrace of love, we find our stance,
Forever entwined, in life's eternal dance.

Farewell, Grandfather

In the quiet corners of memory's hall,
I find your presence, standing tall.
Your laughter echoes in the chambers of my heart,
A melody of love that will never depart.

With each passing day, I feel your absence keen,
A void left behind, where your smile once gleamed.
The warmth of your embrace, now but a fleeting dream,
In the silence of loss, where shadows seem to teem.

You were more than a grandfather, you were a friend,
A guiding light, on whom I could depend.
Your wisdom, a beacon in life's stormy sea,
Now lost to the winds of eternity.

Yet in the depths of sorrow, I find solace too,
In the memories we shared, in the love we knew.
For though you may be gone, your spirit lives on,
In every sunrise, in every dawn.

So farewell, grandfather, though you may be far,
Your love remains, like a guiding star.
In the tapestry of life, your thread still weaves,
In the hearts of those who grieve.